Police Officers
Community Workers

by Alice K. Flanagan

Content Adviser: Bryce D. Kolpack,
Police Executive Research Forum

Reading Adviser: Dr. Linda D. Labbo,
Department of Reading Education, College of Education,
The University of Georgia

COMPASS POINT BOOKS

Minneapolis, Minnesota

Compass Point Books
3109 West 50th Street, #115
Minneapolis, MN 55410

Visit Compass Point Books on the Internet at *www.compasspointbooks.com* or e-mail your
request to *custserv@compasspointbooks.com*

Photographs ©:

FPG International/Michael Nelson, cover; Unicorn Stock Photos/Ronald Lopez, 4; International Stock/Bill Stanton, 5;
Photri-Microstock, 6; Leslie O'Shaughnessy, 7; Visuals Unlimited/A. J. Copley, 8; Shaffer Photography/James L. Shaffer, 9;
Leslie O'Shaughnessy, 10; Photri-Microstock, 11; Leslie O'Shaughnessy, 12; Index Stock Imagery, 13; International Stock/
Scott Campbell, 14; International Stock/Hank Azzato, 15; Leslie O'Shaughnessy, 16, 17; FPG International/Terry Qing, 18;
David F. Clobes, 19; Leslie O'Shaughnessy, 20, 21, 22; International Stock/Jonathan E. Pite, 23; Leslie O'Shaughnessy, 24;
International Stock/Scott Barrow, 25; FPG International/Mark Scott, 26; Shaffer Photography/James L. Shaffer, 27.

Editors: E. Russell Primm and Emily J. Dolbear
Photo Researcher: Svetlana Zhurkina
Photo Selector: Linda S. Koutris
Design: Bradfordesign, Inc.

Library of Congress Cataloging-in-Publication Data

Flanagan, Alice K.
    Police officers / by Alice K. Flanagan.
        p. cm. — (Community workers)
    Includes bibliographical references and index.
    Summary: An introduction to the career of police officer, including the duties, uniforms, equipment,
and their contribution to the community.
    ISBN 0-7565-0011-7 (hardcover)
    ISBN 0-7565-1196-8 (paperback)
        1. Police—Juvenile literature. 2. Police—Vocational guidance—Juvenile literature. [1. Police.
2. Occupations.] I. Title.
    HV7922 .F59 2000
    363.2'023'73—dc21   00-008627

Table of Contents

What Do Police Officers Do?

Police officers work to keep neighborhoods safe. They have a dangerous job. They stop fights and catch **criminals**. Criminals are people who break the law.

A police officer arrests a criminal on the beach.

Catching a criminal in the city

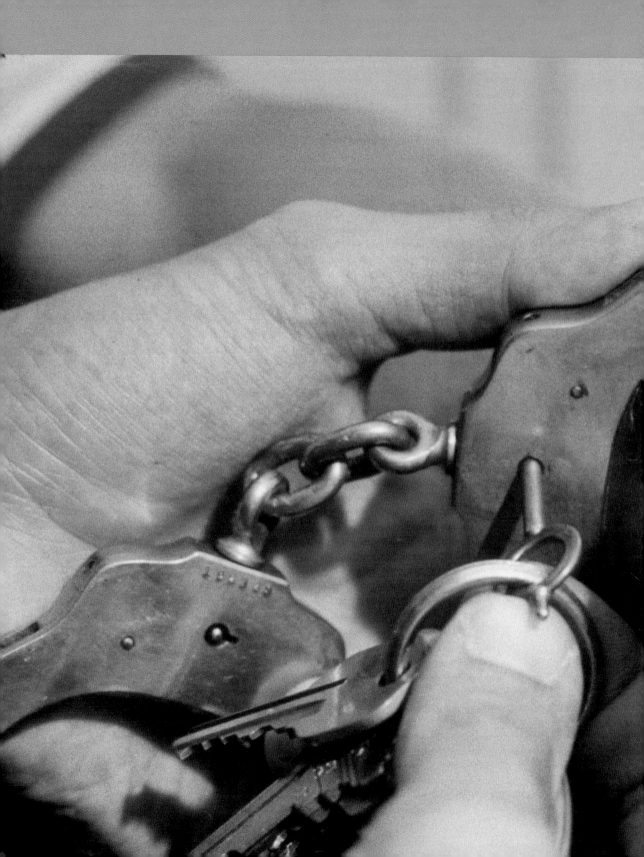

What Tools and Equipment Do They Use?

Police officers use **handcuffs** to control criminals. If police officers cannot talk criminals into giving up, they use force. Sometimes they use a **baton** or **pepper spray**. Police officers use their guns only when they have no other choice.

◀ Handcuffs

Police equipment ▶

How Do Police Officers Help?

Police officers help drivers when accidents happen. They also direct traffic and tell people when it is safe to cross the street. Some police officers try to solve crimes after they have happened. They are called **detectives**.

◀ Directing traffic

A detective at the scene of a crime ▶

Where Do They Work?

Some police officers work on the streets of the neighborhood. Other police officers **patrol** the highway. Some officers patrol parks and mountain areas that are hard to get to by car. They ride horses and are called **mounted police**.

◀ A police officer patrols the highway on a motorcycle.

A park police officer on a horse ▶

Who Do They Work With?

Some police officers work with another officer called a **partner**. Officers rely on people in the community to help them find criminals. Without other people's help, a police officer would not be able to do a good job.

◀ Partners on bicycles

Students in a classroom at police school ▶

What Do They Wear?

Most police officers wear uniforms, name tags, and badges. Officers who do not wear uniforms are called undercover officers. They do not want people to know they are police officers because they want to catch criminals in the act.

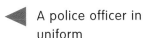

A police officer in uniform

A police badge, or shield

What Training Does It Take?

People who want to be police officers must finish high school and sometimes college. Then they train at a police school. They learn about the law and first aid. They learn how to write reports, solve problems, and fire guns. They also learn how to protect themselves and other people.

◀ Students in a classroom at police school

A police officer ▶ practices shooting.

What Skills Do They Need?

Police officers must be able to think fast. Sometimes they have to stop a fight. Sometimes they have to calm people down. Often, their words are the best weapons they have.

A police officer writes down a statement from a criminal

A police officer explains a ticket to a driver.

Police officers also need good speaking and writing skills. They talk to a lot of people and write a lot of reports. Police officers also need good math skills. They take measurements when they try to solve crimes or describe traffic accidents.

◀ Taking measurements at a crime scene

Writing reports ▶

What Problems Do They Face?

Police officers must be willing to work in dangerous places. Every day, they must solve problems. And police departments must have officers on duty every hour of every day.

◀ A rescue team climbs a wall.

Police officers try to keep ▶ crowds orderly.

Would You Like to Be a Police Officer?

Do you like to help others? Do you like to do what is right? Maybe you would like to be a police officer someday. You can prepare now. In school, follow the rules. Help others and learn how to solve problems.

A police officer in a classroom

A police officer helps a boy cross the street.

A Police Officer's Tools and Clothes

radio

shoulder patch

computer

uniform

A Police Officer's Day

Early morning
- The police officer arrives at the police station early in the morning.
- She meets with other officers to receive the day's orders.
- About 10:00 A.M., the police officer visits a school to talk to children about safe neighborhoods.

Noon
- The police officer patrols the neighborhood on foot with her partner.
- After lunch, she writes a parking ticket for a car parked in front of a fire hydrant.
- She also gives directions to someone who is lost.

Afternoon
- Then, the police officer sees someone who may be stealing from a house.
- She calls the station on her radio and chases the man running from the house.
- She catches him and puts handcuffs on him.
- Then, she calls the station for help.

Evening
- After a police car takes the man to the station, the police officer returns to the station to fill out forms.

Night
- At the end of a long day, the police officer has to sign out.

Glossary

baton—a heavy wooden stick

criminals—people who have broken the law

detectives—police officers who look for clues and talk to people who might have seen a criminal break the law

handcuffs—metal rings that lock around a prisoner's wrists

mounted police—police officers who patrol on horses

partner—the person a police officer works with

patrol—to walk around an area to protect it

pepper spray—a liquid that stings the skin and eyes; police officers may use it to stop criminals

Did You Know?

- About 70 to 80 percent of a police officer's day is spent with people who are not criminals.

- Police officers wear shoulder patches only in North America.

- More than 604,000 men and women work as full-time police officers in the United States.

- The first police force was started in London in 1829.

Want to Know More?

At the Library

Flanagan, Alice K., and Christine Osinski (photographer). *Officer Brown Keeps Neighborhoods Safe*. Danbury Conn.: Children's Press, 1998.

Schomp, Virginia. *If You Were a Police Officer*. New York: Benchmark Books, 1998.

Winkleman, Katherine K., and John S. Winkleman (illustrator). *Police Patrol*. New York: Walker and Co., 1996.

On the Web

Police Guide

http://www.policeguide.com/

For a guide to law-enforcement memorabilia

Super Trooper

http://www.users.fast.net/~louis2/index.html

For information about police officers' equipment and safety tips

Through the Mail

Fraternal Order of Police

2100 Gardiner Lane

Louisville, KY 40205

For information about police careers

On the Road

The Federal Bureau of Investigation

J. Edgar Hoover Building

935 Pennsylvania Avenue, N.W.

Washington, DC 20535-0001

For an informative tour about law enforcement and the FBI

Index

About the Author

Alice K. Flanagan writes books for children and teachers. Since she was a young girl, she has enjoyed writing. Today, she has published more than seventy books on a wide variety of topics. Some of the books she has written include biographies of U.S. presidents and first ladies; biographies of people working in neighborhoods; phonics books for beginning readers; informational books about birds and Native Americans; and career education in the classroom. Alice K. Flanagan lives in Chicago, Illinois.